Your Self-empowerment GPS

Your guide for achieving personal greatness.

Dare to be You; Dare to Love Yourself

Greg Pirio

Copyright © 2020 Greg Pirio

Table of Contents

Introduction

You will find herein a guide for your personal journey of self-empowerment.

This guide is a companion to the book *Outside Eden's Gate: The Secrets of Self-empowerment*, written by Greg Pirio.

The down-to-earth activities contained in the guide will increase your understanding of your situation and enable you to leave behind habits and beliefs that limit you from creating a more fulfilled life of your own choosing. The guide is designed to help you realize the incredible creative potential that already exists within you. You have the ingredients for personal greatness; you are beautiful, brilliant, and worthy of love.

The accumulation of personal power should be at the core of everyone's life journey. It's a choice everyone has to make. We can choose to remain in self-limiting paradigms, or we can embrace attitudes, beliefs, and behaviors that are self-empowering and lead us to personal greatness.

We can use a variety of terms to describe personal power such as confidence, courage, and competence. People acquire these constructive and other qualities in the course of their personal development by leaving behind behaviors and attitudes they evolved as children and by acquiring healthier, more fulfilling life strategies. The Self-empowerment GPS will guide you on this journey of self-realization through the creation of new beliefs, thought patterns, and habits that will increase your personal greatness.

The Self-empowerment GPS asks you to "Dare to be You" and to "Dare to Love Yourself." As you will discover as you follow this course, the ultimate secret of personal empowerment is self-love. Being able to sense one's inner worthiness, brilliance, and beauty makes it easier to love oneself. This course is designed to make you realize the magnificence that is already you. Many good things will inevitably flow from this realization as you radiate your beauty, brilliance, and self-love into the world.

How to Use the Self-empowerment GPS

Each weekly exercise in this guide consists of a secret presented in the *Outside Eden's Gate: The Secrets of Self-empowerment* book followed by several questions and activities designed to encourage your adoption of more powerful beliefs and habits critical to self-empowerment.

You may reflect on the secrets and respond to the accompanying exercises at your own pace and in your own way. You may want to choose one secret a week during a nine-month period. During this period, you will become witness to the incubation of a more powerful and more centered you. If, at any time, you feel it is difficult to find the answers to the questions you will find, don't be concerned. Keep at the exercises, and you will inevitably see a more empowered you evolve.

The secrets and exercises are designed to reinforce your learning experience and to help you develop new skills and habits that create a more joy-filled and peaceful you. You will find different exercises will be repeating some of the core concepts in different ways. This is intentional, as your current state of habitual thinking took root in your psyche through the repetition of thoughts. It is likewise through repetition that you will learn to imbue yourself with new, more empowering habitual thoughts.

The design of a nine-month period for this activity is no accident. It is inspired symbolically by the time required for incubation of human life and suggests with patience and dedication you can give birth to a more empowered you. Oh, and be patient with the process. Over time, you will gain greater insights as a genuine and authentic you incubates.

You can follow the Self-empowerment GPS solo, that is, by yourself, or you may take it with trusted friends who can give you feedback, enhance your insights, and give you encouragement. In a group, everyone can discuss their responses to the questions and suggested activities.

If you are taking this journey solo or as a member in a group, it may be most helpful to write your responses in a journal, whether handwritten or digitized. And, don't hesitate to come back to an exercise and your written reflections during subsequent weeks. This will stimulate further discovery and understanding as you progress down your path of personal self-empowerment.

I guarantee you that at the end of nine months, if you hold course, you can return to the first secrets and see with incredible clarity the progress you have made. You will have an appreciation of what you have accomplished by letting go of self-limiting beliefs and behaviors. You will discover and embrace your personal power measured in terms of confidence, competence, courage, and compassion for self and others.

Accept this challenge, and **"dare to be you."**

Chapter ONE: The Awakened Life: Secrets for Fulfilling Your Potential

1. **Secret Number 1:** Accept that death awaits all of us. A focus on our mortality is not morose. Indeed, it is liberating. Acknowledgment of our inevitable mortality is a powerful tool to catalyze a personal awakening about the urgency for positive change and to access the energy required to productively move forward on life's journey. Accepting the inevitability of your death is also a call to assume responsibility for the present. So, don't waste a moment of life in complacency or fear of change.

   Fears become insignificant and lose their sway over us when we accept death is always awaiting us. So, be daring in your choices, and never fear the call to adopt change. Change always reflects the passing of something—a type of death—but always with the prospect of a rebirth. Assume responsibility for your rebirth.

   a. If you were on your deathbed, what regrets would you have about the life you have lived? Write them down in a list.

b. Name some actions you have put off from doing although you know it is in your interest to carry them out. Write them down.

c. Ask yourself why you held yourself back from acting in your own interest. What have you feared? Be specific in describing what you feared might happen for each of these actions that you have put off from doing.

d. With this new understanding of what might be holding you back, write down the steps for each of these actions that you can take to assume the responsibility for yourself you have failed to take in the past.

e. If you find it difficult to answer these questions, don't be discouraged. You are at the beginning. Subsequent steps in this GPS guide are designed to help you to more clearly perceive your feelings and see the path forward.

2. **Secret Number Two:** Self-pity and blaming are disempowering. Self-pity, that is, feeling sorry for yourself, is debilitating as it prevents you from taking actions and from assuming personal responsibility for your fate. Accepting personal responsibility for your situations allows you to walk through the door a personal awakening presents to you.

   A personal awakening occurs when something happens in your life to wake you up as if you have been in a slumber. In such a moment, you will realize you must move forward to live a more fulfilled life even if you don't yet know the steps that will be necessary. Don't fret, this understanding will come.

   Accepting personal responsibility rather than blaming others or engaging in self-pity builds the foundation for taking advantage of such awakenings. Taking responsibility enables you to achieve an enriched and powerful life as you become victim no more. This is a potent lesson. Become master of your own destiny by no longer wasting time blaming others or feeling sorry for yourself.

Write down your responses to the following questions:

   a. Name a recent or past instance when you have felt sorry for yourself. Ask yourself what did assuming such an attitude accomplish for you?

b. Ask yourself who in your life is undermining you.

c. How does blaming this other person(s) hold you back?

d. Then ask yourself what would taking responsibility for your situation look like. Write it down. What beliefs about yourself do you think you have to change?

e. Focus on what you can do to change your situation rather than blaming. Write down the actions you will take rather than blaming.

f. What will such a world look and feel like to you once you assume responsibility and initiate the actions you have identified? Write down what you envisage such a world to be like and the feelings you will experience leading a life of your own choosing and making.

g. If you are fearful about undertaking these actions, don't worry. Fear is normal when you venture into unchartered territory, outside of your familiar comfort zone. This course is designed to help you become more courageous so that you can dare to be the true you.

3. **Secret Number Three:** Emotional dependency is the habit of looking to others for answers, validation, and happiness instead of finding our inner direction. The journey of self-empowerment is about reclaiming a sense of innate worthiness, so we trust and value that which comes from within. In achieving this, we become emotionally self-reliant.

   In achieving heightened emotional self-reliance, you will accumulate greater strength, confidence, and competency over time. The achievement of emotional self-reliance will enable you to enhance your self-assertiveness in dealings with other people, to become more discriminating, to make more prudent choices, and to experience a natural, healthy connection with others. And, of course, self-reliance enables you to be more discriminating of the company you keep and of the advice you receive from others.

   a. Have you hoped for a rescue or an escape from an onerous feeling or an emotional predicament? Name some examples of this.

   b. Did you believe another person would provide you with relief from anxiety and more generally the lack of joy you felt? Who was/were that person/those persons?

   c. Take a quiet moment and reflect to what you felt while hoping someone would provide a rescue from onerous feelings.

d. Would you describe the feeling of hoping for a rescue as empowering, or did it put you in a weakened state?

e. Can you point to a time or moment when you felt powerful, that is, when the decisions you made and the actions you took would bring about positive change? When did that happen? What did that feel like?

f. How might you recapture that feeling of a more powerful you if you have left that feeling of empowerment behind?

g. Can you imagine what it might be like if you brought a more powerful, less dependent you into all your relationships? Describe what that imagined life would look like and what it would feel like.

h. If this thought of becoming more powerful makes you feel a little afraid, be patient. Little by little, the world of a more empowered you will be revealed and your inner joy and peace will abound. Imagine yourself in such a world. Describe it in detail. Describe how you would be different. Describe the new you that is in the making. Write this in your journal.

4. **Secret Number Four:** There are blessings to be found in seemingly onerous situations, particularly when we can look beyond feeling sorry for ourselves and assume responsibility. Self-pity—this feeling sorry for ourselves that is often triggered when we experience pain or discomfort—inevitably blinds us from seeing the full richness of the present moment. That used to be how I reacted to the world of seeming problems, that is, with a "poor me" attitude.

   Self-pity, this sense of victimhood, deprives us of personal power and tends to focus our attention on negativity, thus blinding us to the rich potential that exists in any given situation or moment. Engaging in self-pity leads to a focus on disappointments instead of on the opportunities presented. Self-pity also leads to a preoccupation with fear and undermines our self-confidence.

   Self-pity also means handing over power to others. Remember, we are only victims if we allow it. Respond to any untoward situation knowing you are master of your own destiny if you so allow.

   Let go of self-pity, and your stores of personal power will increase. You will more easily see the rich untapped possibilities that lie in every moment. You will be victim no more.

   Abandoning self-pity is an awesome act of self-love.

a. Look back on events in your recent past when you felt sorry for yourself. List them in your journal.

b. Indeed, is there something going on right now in your life that you react to by feeling sorry for yourself? Describe how you feel about that situation.

c. Are you blaming others for your perceived misfortune? Who might that be? Then ask yourself what you gain by handing over your power to him, her, or them.

d. Then, take some ten minutes of seated quiet meditation to ponder this situation and the self-pity you may be experiencing. Focus on your breath coming in and out. Feel your belly and chest move in and out as you breathe. Focus on the confidence that emerges as you appreciate this life-giving force of breath that dwells within you. Understand that the inner you is where your real strength comes from.

e. In this moment, commit to stop blaming others for pain or discomfort. Assume responsibility for all, just as you assume responsibility for breathing. Keep breathing. On your in breath take in and accept your pain; on your out breath, expand your self-confidence, strength, and empowerment into your world.

f. Ponder what steps you will take to change this situation as you assume responsibility. Then when you end this meditative session, write down what actions you will take to change your situation. You will surely see a different landscape, and opportunities will become more visible to you.

g. In the future, whenever you feel stuck in a bad situation, focus on your breath. Breathe in your pain. Breathe out your power. You are now transforming your world by accepting the discomfort and abandoning the old habit of self-pity.

5. **Secret Number Five:** When we are stuck, that is, when we fail to take action to improve our situation or exit from a bad one, life will inevitably shake us up with a personal crisis of intense magnitude. Be prepared to accept such moments that feel like a personal crisis as opportunities. You can learn great lessons from such moments if you embrace the fear and other pain you may feel in those moments. It is in the embrace of the discomfort of these moments that we can discover truths that ultimately empower us. Embrace discomfort with patience, and your personal power will undoubtedly grow and your suffering will lessen.

   a. Do you run away from discomfort? Describe at least one negative or caustic set of circumstances you ignored to your own peril.

   b. What sort of story were you telling yourself that prevented you from taking concrete action to end up on better or more neutral ground? What did you fear would happen if you took some action to improve your situation?

   c. In hindsight, how would you change the story you were telling yourself about your future that kept you stuck in a bad situation? What were you fearing if you were to make a change?

   d. What sort of positive feeling or belief about

yourself would have empowered you to get unstuck and embrace change? Describe what a more empowered you would have done in such a situation?

e. Identify an area in your life right now where you may be resisting the inner call for change. Take a quiet moment and ask yourself what you are fearing. What can you tell yourself in a loving way to give you the courage to take actions that you need to take? Remember never to berate yourself. Always think about how to be moving forward in a self-loving way. You deserve the best. We all deserve the best.

f. List some of the actions you can take to change this situation.

6. **Secret Number Six:** Being stuck in a disempowering belief system is no fun as we constantly replay negative thoughts and feelings that take their toll on our health and well-being. However, being stuck can also be a harbinger of new self-liberating possibilities. Remember to look at the duality of a given experience! The seeming onerous is pregnant with new possibilities.

   Your beliefs can hold you back and keep you stuck, so understanding them will provide you with insight on how to move forward. Describing the belief system that holds you back will help to liberate you as you increase your understanding of why you may be clinging to negative situations. These could be a negative relationship, a harmful workplace environment, or any situation that just plainly undermines your confidence and sense of worthiness. Acknowledging the beliefs that hold you back is an important step in reclaiming your power. Realizing you are stuck is good and normal for growth and for the accumulation of personal power. However, staying stuck is debilitating. So, be glad that you are acknowledging that you have been stuck.

Flipping the switch from viewing moments of personal angst as a penalty or a punishment to viewing such moments as a trigger for change and a sign of good things to come is empowering.

a. Do you feel stuck in some aspect of your life? How? In your journal, describe the ways your thoughts about yourself may have created this "stuck" place.

b. Describe what your life would look life if you got unstuck and could change this aspect of your life into something positive—a place where your natural and innate sense of joy would fill you up. How would that feel? Describe those feelings in detail. Look at yourself as worthy of love and deserving of respect. How would you honor this wonderful, amazing person you are? Write down the things you would do to honor yourself.

c. Imagine what it would feel like to be that more empowered you? You may want to refer to the Hallmarks of an Empowered Person Table to stimulate your creativity. The table can be found at http://gregpirio.com/acquiring-personal-power-is-healthy-and-wise/.

d. Exercise responsibility. What steps might you take to be the person you want to be, to claim the life that is your dream? Write these steps down and then make your plans to accomplish these steps. Implementing these steps will be milestones on your life's journey. It's okay to take baby steps at first. What might these be? Your confidence will grow as you take the steps. Don't be hesitant!

7. **Secret Number Seven:** A healthy sense of self-worth acts as an antidote to the fear of change as one has the confidence to know the much sought-after feelings of joy and peace already exist within and do not come from without. So, in giving value to self through the act of self-love, we learn over time that these most precious of feelings are an inherent part of our beautiful essence. Despite whatever change may occur around us, we always have recourse to this essence that eternally exists within each one of us. Tapping into these feelings and maintaining a connection to them are incredible acts of personal empowerment. As this happens, one's personal power increases. Internalizing the secrets offered in this book provides a transformative pathway to achieving authentic self-love.

   a. Take five minutes of quiet meditation. Remind yourself of the frequent personal fears you have identified in the course of your GPS Self-empowerment journey. List them in your journal.

   b. Can you feel these fears and their pain without seeking to escape them? What is the worst thing, if any, to have befallen you when you have allowed uncomfortable feelings since you began this journey? What benefits have you derived by acknowledging fears and not acting on them?

   c. Now think of someone you personally know who may be operating out of a place of fear. What about their behavior makes you feel that they are operating from a place of fear? Can you imagine what event might have given rise to their fearful thoughts, or what is the source of their doubts about their worthiness?

d. Write this person a letter, without sending it, telling him/her you understand his/her fears and to tell him/her you wished she/he understood his/her intrinsic lovability?

8. **Secret Number Eight:** Dependency on another is most of all a habit of the mind; it is a habitual approach to confronting problems in which we look outside the self for acceptance and approval instead of finding our own inner direction. You can change your habit of looking to others for acceptance and approval, just as you can change negative habits like chewing your fingernails, picking your nose, or rushing to the refrigerator to eat something to comfort you when you are anxious. A commitment to change a negative habit takes confidence, and this you will accumulate as you become increasingly empowered.

What we call romantic love is so often nothing more than the habit of intimacy with another, and this form of dependency becomes especially evident when the other person is a source of negativity. Real love is a healthy connection between people, not dependence.

If you feel stuck in a bad relationship, bring all the emotional turmoil you are caught up in down to something mundane and manageable—just recognize it as another one of your bad habits you need to change. Then, turn inward and acknowledge your personal beauty, brilliance, and self-worth. In so doing, your inner wisdom will reveal itself, and you will know how to proceed.

If you are stuck in a bad relationship, just remind yourself to be free of your sense of dependency and to gain in your personal power all you have to do is break a bad habit.

a. Describe at least one instance of emotional dependence on another that you have experienced. Did you hand over your power to this other person? How?

b. How might your life be different if you operated from a place of emotional self-reliance rather than from emotional dependence? It is important to remember the journey of self-empowerment is about reclaiming a sense of innate worthiness so you trust and value that which comes from within. In achieving this, you will become emotionally self-reliant.

c. How would you describe the difference between love and dependence?

d. Write down some thoughts or stories you tell yourself that are blocking you from appreciating your own self-worth. How would you change this self-talk to feel more whole by yourself?

e. Write down three statements that would express love for yourself as if you were a loving parent talking to a child to encourage him/her or as if you

were a genuine lover appreciating you and the glory
that is you.

9. **Secret Number Nine:** When you experience uncomfortable emotions, it is best to just sit with them rather than reacting by seeking an escape from the fear or other forms of discomfort. In so doing, the energy of the discomfort is neutralized in this act of patience. We can then mold this freed energy into creative forces. Practice this skill, and you will learn to transform the energy of anger into the resolve to change your circumstances, the energy of fear into self-compassion and confidence, and the energy of shame into self-worth. In so doing, you will become the master of your own destiny. You will become a courageous person.

    a. Name something that causes you anxiety. How do you typically respond to an anxious feeling? Describe this in your journal.

    b. What would be the worst thing that would happen to you if you did not divert yourself from a feeling of fear or anxiety, that is, if you accepted the negative feeling? Describe what you imagine that worst thing to be.

    c. The next time you feel anxious, do nothing. As soon as possible, find a quiet place to sit and just experience the feeling. Examine it as if you were looking at a piece of art in a museum. Imagine it as an object outside of yourself you don't have to push away. It will begin to lose its hold on you.

d. With practice, you can use this technique to develop a new habitual way of responding to emotional discomfort. Indeed, by not seeking to escape from such feelings but rather by embracing them, you will begin learning a new habit--a habit of choosing how to respond to discomfort. The new habit you will be adopting is "courage." Write down how an increasingly courageous you would respond to a common fear that you experience? Describe this fear and how you would act from your place of courage. Describe the steps—the feelings and thoughts—you go through when acting courageously before fear and other uncomfortable emotions.

10. **Secret Number Ten:** Pushing distasteful feelings underground and out of sight has profound implications. First and foremost, it means you become disconnected from feeling. All emotions are okay. Don't be afraid of them; they are a key part of our intelligence and the human experience.

Avoiding feelings is perilous as you turn your attention to external influences and adopt behaviors prescribed by others. You don't want to lose track of the authentic you, substituting your authentic creativity with formulas for living defined by others. Treasure what comes from within you as you learn to accept all your feelings.

So, stay with the uncomfortable and let it dissipate. You don't want to fall into the trap of seeking false security from external sources; this reliance on external sources cuts you off from the awesome creative potential that lies within you and the power to imagine a different way of being in this world that is on your own terms. To strengthen your power to create a world of your own imagination, savor that which causes discomfort and witness the creative potential that emerges from the acceptance of discomforting feelings. Oh, and be sure to smile as your personal power grows.

Practice the art of genuine feeling to nourish a habit of imagination and creativity.

a. When you experience an uncomfortable feeling, refrain from diversion as a way of seeking escape from it. What does that feel like to just stay with the uncomfortable feeling?

b. Describe an instance when you caved into fear and failed to follow your own instincts.

c. Imagine now how events might have unfolded differently if you didn't give in to your fears. Write down how you felt and why and then how different your life might have been if you had not limited yourself.

d. Have you been afraid of what others might think about you? Are you avoiding an inconvenient truth or difficult emotion? Discover your own truth, and don't be afraid to step outside of the box.

e. The next time you are fearful, don't act on the feeling. Go for a leisurely walk. Savor what emerges. Remind yourself that uncomfortable feelings can never hurt you. In allowing all feelings, a truer and more intended course of action will be revealed to you. Count on it. Write down what ideas emerge. These will become part of your vision for a future you.

f. Experiencing nature can awaken in you a sense of vitality and infinity, setting you on a path to discovering and unleashing your core creativity. Without conscious thought, you can look up at the astonishing number of stars in the sky or at the leaves on a single tree and feel a sense of vastness and spaciousness. Try this.

As you gaze at the heavens the ancients also observed, contemplate how humanity throughout history and across continents has pondered these very stars. You will experience being part of something larger than yourself, and you will feel as if it has always existed and always will if you are open to the moment. Feel the personal power that comes from this sense of connection. Describe this experience in your journal. Allow a healthy connection to your feelings and to nature to be expressed.

11. **Secret Number Eleven:** Imagination is central both to creating the life you want and to allowing yourself to be the authentic you. You are capable of imagining how you wish to make your contribution in this world.

Imagining a fulfilling life is the first step in this process. You then take the idea you have dared to see in your head and transform it into something real. Your personal genius creates the imagined vision. Then, the transformation of your genius's handiwork into a reality is your creativity. Your creativity takes the vision—your dream—and turns it into a reality.

Creativity is required to transform your purposeful dream into a masterful work of art that is your life. Holding true to this process will empower you with intentions, habits, and the will needed to be a creator. Have the courage and perseverance to make your vision a reality. It is your responsibility and no one else's. (And stick with the Self-empowerment GPS. It is designed to help you strengthen your imagination and creativity.)

a. Set aside time every day this week for imagining the life you want to create—a life filled with joy or peace or confidence or whatever positive feeling you may perceive as lacking now but which you want to characterize the life you are creating. This is <u>not</u> about hoping for something new. This is about creating something new. Imagining is the first step in unleashing your creative process.

b. A surefire method for tapping into your authentic imagination is to recall how worthy and lovable you are. Recognizing your innate value and lovability as a person is the key to personal empowerment. Acknowledging your value and lovability will fuel your imagination. So, give yourself the gift of a quiet meditative moment reflecting on your essential beauty and goodness, and describe in a few lines how adorable you are. This is like writing a short love letter to yourself to help release your imagination's vital juices.

c. Then, write down things a lovable person like you deserves in your life. On one day this week, you may focus on the type of relationship(s) you may want in your life. How do you imagine your friends, a special romantic person, your coworkers, etcetera to be? Imagine how you want others to treat you and how you will also treat others. Write down what you deserve and expect.

d. On another day, you may wish to imagine how you want to have fun. It might be hiking in the wilderness, picking up seashells on an isolated beach, painting a picture, taking photographs, playing soccer, skydiving, cultivating a vegetable garden, reading an inspiring book, going to a concert, or playing a game of cards with friends. Write down a list of the fun things that you want to bring into your life. Don't worry about being realistic. Asking yourself what is realistic is like a curse meant to destroy your ability to dream. Remember your creativity will make your dreams a reality. Write down how engaging in your fun activity will make you feel.

e. On yet another day, imagine the productive activity you might want to engage in. It might be about a career you imagine pursuing, about what type of parent you want to be, or about what type of volunteer activity you might engage in. You choose. Then, describe what you would be doing. Imagine how this would make you feel.

f. Now indulge in some creativity. Take one of the dreams you have imagined—be it about relationships, fun, or your productive activity—and write down a list of actions you will take to make that dream your reality. These actions are the steps that will lead you to the destination you have imagined. Then choose a date by which you intend to reach your destination.

12. **Secret Number Twelve:** Immerse yourself in artistic exploration to ignite your creativity. Don't just be a consumer of knowledge and art. Also be their creator. As a parent, I shifted from reading bedtime stories to my kids to telling them original stories and having them participate in the creation of the nighttime storytelling. Likewise, I encouraged them to draw rather than to use coloring books. I asked myself, "Why should they fill in with color the lines that other people have drawn?" I gave them permission to draw their own lines. We draw the lines of our life whether we are conscious of what we are doing or not.

I made this switch to oblige them to exercise their imaginative faculties and encourage creativity. It works for children, and it works for adults. All of us are more than consumers of the works of others. Be a creator, and enrich your life and the world around you.

a. Write down a list of activities you would want to perform if you didn't watch TV or spend so much time absorbed by social media. These could include writing, drawing, cooking, gardening, sculpting, sports, political activities, or any other imaginative and creative activity that feels good to you.

b. Now imagine how undertaking the activities you have chosen might impact your life when you perform them? How might your life be enriched by them? Write your imaginings down in your journal.

c. Then disconnect your TV cable or turn off your TV
    and give yourself a break from social media. If
    others in your household are watching TV, excuse
    yourself and go into another room or away from
    your home to perform the activities you have
    written down.

d. Begin with the intent, and then take steps to making
    creativity a regular companion in your life even if
    these are baby steps. Don't worry about failure.
    There is no such thing as failure when you create
    from a place of self-acceptance and self-love. There
    may be self-doubt or insecurity, but acceptance of
    these feeling leads to strength and confidence. That
    is for sure!

e. If you choose art as a creative endeavor, you may
    want to consider getting Betty Edwards's book
    Drawing from the Right Side of the Brain. Her
    methods can be truly inspirational.

13. **Secret Number Thirteen:** To be an imaginatively resourceful and creative person, regard life as an interesting game that is fun to play. Be courageous, feeling that life has very few missteps that cannot be remedied and challenges that cannot be overcome. Indeed, we all can learn from challenging situations, and that is an essential part of the journey of empowerment.

Abandon the idea of failure. There is no such thing as failure; there is only learning from your efforts, whether they yield the results you had in mind or not. The key to switching from a belief in failure to a more wholehearted approach that values creativity and learning is to refrain from questioning your self-worth. Check my essay "Beyond Success and Failure" to further understand the mythology surrounding success and failure. The essay can be found at: www.gregpirio.com

Adopting such a stance fuels your sense of confidence and allows you to see all sorts of opportunities that emerge along the route you have set for yourself. Excessively focusing on a preconceived idea of what success will look like is similar to putting on blinders that prevent you from seeing the unfolding of new opportunities. So, please proceed with a sense of confidence. And, be lighthearted about it all. Enjoy the ride!

a. The previous week you were encouraged to refrain from TV watching and reducing time on social media, write in your journal about the feelings that come up during the time you have freed up for other activities.

b. Describe what it feels like to perform the creative activities you previously indicated you would like to be performing but had no time for. Contentment? Joy? Fear? Whatever you feel is okay. Feeling is an end in itself.

At times, you will experience discomfort as you are no longer distracted from your feelings. Be patient with any difficult feelings that come up. This is an almost inevitable part of the process of self-empowering, learning to be at ease with feelings that may have been difficult in the past. Persist. You will reap a tremendous reward.

c. Plan the creative activities you would like to pursue and the steps you would need to take to realize them. Write these steps down.

d. Now, set up a calendar for when you will begin undertaking them, and keep with them. If you don't complete them as you planned, don't feel bad about it; encourage yourself and remind yourself you are changing habits that have accumulated over years.

Always treat yourself in a loving way. You're awesome!

33

14. **Secret Number Fourteen:** If you've set yourself out on a path in life that now looks like a blunder to you, don't even begin to lament, first of all, because there isn't anything whatsoever you can do to change what has already happened. And, secondly and most importantly, all your experiences are rich with lessons ripe for the picking. Seize upon them, and let them nourish you. Imagine how the future will look differently because you are learning from what seemed like a negative, and release your creativity to make a newly imagined reality become your future.

    a. Now that you are taking baby steps toward leading a more creative life, you will likely be forging a new vision of and gaining new perspectives on the life that you want to be living. Keep up those creative activities you have embarked upon that give you a sense of joy and well-being even if you feel scared at times by this course of action. Your creative impulses will serve you in all aspects of your life.

    b. With this new creative trajectory underway, think of something you have thought of as a misstep in your life, asking yourself what lessons are embedded in it. Instead of lamenting or blaming, you are using your energy in a creative way by exploring the lesson hidden in each moment. For instance, you might have learned to surround yourself by loving people who display a sense of gratitude.

Here are some questions that may be helpful as you are determined to turn the "negative" into a "positive." You can pick out a negative event, and write answers to these questions in your journal.

    i. What happened that felt negative?
    ii. What did I learn from this?
    iii. What could I do differently the next time?
    iv. What will I likely gain by behaving differently? List them.

c. Now choose another example of what was a misstep in your life, and draw out one or more lessons from that event. Make a list of the lessons learned and describe how you intend to incorporate each one of them into your life. As you proceed on your journey, these lessons will become clearer, and you will grow in your personal power as you put into practice what you have learned.

15. Secret Number Fifteen: We all have an innate urge to feel a sense of connection or belonging with others. We can get very accustomed to turning to one or more people for a sense of connection or belonging. When relationships are supportive and healthy, the connection should be valued. However, there are times when we may be the object of disrespect, abuse, and/or manipulation in a relationship.

If you are experiencing a negative relationship somewhere in your life, acknowledge it as a bad habit. Breaking such a bad habit doesn't have to be that hard. Minimize its significance by thinking of it like another trivial, even comical, bad habit like picking your nose. This is one way of making change easier. Remember it is important to be lighthearted about serious stuff. Things don't have to be so dark because of the light that eternally dwells within you.

a. Write in your journal about the healthy relationships you have in your life and what makes them healthy. Breathe deeply when you ponder the behaviors and attitudes displayed by these people to help you focus on the positive feelings these relationships promote in you. Write down what you might say to these supportive people to thank them. Tell them specifically what they do that causes you to feel good about yourself.

b. Name those individuals who are having a negative influence in your life, and ask yourself why you tolerate unhealthy relationships. How might you treat these relationships if you were acting toward yourself in a self-loving way?

c. Choose one of these negative people, and write a letter to him/her, describing how their behavior negatively affects you and how you prefer to be treated. Don't feel like you have to give the person that letter. This is a practice for setting healthy boundaries as a way of loving yourself.

d. For more ideas on how to precisely and effectively set boundaries with others, check out http://www.oprah.com/spirit/Begin-to-Set-Personal-Boundaries_1/3

e. Remember this exercise is not about blaming the other. It is about admitting to yourself how you might allow negativity into your life so that you may take responsibility in correcting onerous situations. Name three things you might do differently as part of accepting responsibility to develop wholesome relationships.

16. **Secret Number Sixteen:** To cultivate self-loving, start your day with something that is an act of loving kindness. I did this by waking up earlier than normal and painting, writing in a journal, or practicing yoga instead of rushing to answer urgent emails from clients. I used to leave the painting until late at night when I was too tired to be truly creative. Despite my resolve to start my day with an act of loving kindness to myself, sometimes, I fall short and rush to meet a deadline. But there will always be deadlines.

When I start my day with art, journal writing, or yoga, the entire day turns more magical. Instead of perceiving emails from a stressful perspective, I then view them as opportunities to contribute to the world through sincere engagement.

a. Choose to begin the day with an act of self-love; it could be a leisurely walk, cooking a special dish, a calming yoga session, or writing in the journal you have started as part of Self-empowerment GPS, or maybe it will consist of ten minutes of quiet meditation. You decide what works for you.

b. After doing this for several days, reflect on how different this has made you feel. Write down your observations to help you remember the advantages you have incurred and the value of making this new behavior a positive habit. Remember to always treat yourself to the gift of loving kindness.

17. **Secret Number Seventeen:** One way to enhance your emotional self-reliance is to learn the practice of forgiveness. If you are unable to forgive another for his/her violations or wrongdoings, you stay stuck in a state of unintended dysfunctional dependency on the violator. Forgiving another frees you from the bitterness, anger, and even vengeful impulses you have stored up toward the one whom you perceived as having wronged you. Forgiving helps to give you a clear head and peaceful heart as you move forward. Forgiveness doesn't mean you deny the other person's responsibility for violating trust or mistreating you, and it doesn't minimize or justify the wrong. You can forgive the person without excusing the act.

Equally important is forgiving yourself for the abuse, large or small, you have allowed because of a pattern of unsupportive personal beliefs. Self-forgiveness provides the opportunity to let go of blame, shame, and guilt around your behavior and beliefs. Self-forgiveness sets the stage for creating different, more positive behaviors based on a new way of being and believing. Both directions of forgiveness—outbound and inbound—are acts of love to yourself.

a. Name one or two people toward whom you hold anger, and describe what they did to make you angry. (Remember that it's preferable not to act impulsively from a place of anger. Sit with the feeling, and choose how you want to respond with a cool mind.)

b. Write a letter to one of them, forgiving them for their behavior. In the letter, mention what the person did to wrong you; acknowledge the other person's own limited evolution by describing how you imagine the person's own injurious past contributed to his/her aggression, and wish that person the courage to heal and grow in her/his own personal power. You don't need to send the letter. Just use it to open a new chapter in the book of your life.

c. Now write a letter to yourself, forgiving yourself for having allowed this other person into your life or for having not kept the person at a distance once you became aware of his/her toxicity. Then, thank yourself for having learned some important lessons. List these lessons in your letter.

d. Now just write a short letter forgiving everyone for just being human and blemished. Wish everyone enlightenment, evolution, and healthy personal empowerment.

18. **Secret Number Eighteen:** When you allow your imagination to run free, you enrich the world with your brilliance. If, on the other hand, you adopt a formula for righteous living, you eclipse your imagination by following a formula, and as a result, you impoverish the world by not adding to its wealth of creative ideas and authenticity. When you don't allow your own imagination its freedom, you produce sameness and conformity. The more you feel self-worth and self-love, the greater the power of your imagination to release positive energy into the world is. When you feel your own worthiness and achieve greater emotional self-reliance, then creativity, which is a built-in attribute of each us, will take shape and form.

The exercise of imagination is a display of one's inherent powers regardless of whether the envisioned external change is brought about as expected. But, have confidence your world will change for the better. As you step forward in accordance to what you have imagined, additional pathways you had not yet imagined will open to you like magic. This is an inevitable product of authentic thought and action. So, be on the lookout for pleasant surprises.

a. As a warm-up, describe what makes you worthy of love and belonging.

b. Now from the recognition of your innate lovability, imagine how you would like your life to be including the types of relationships you would like to have and the types of productive activities you would like to engage in. Write these down to help remember them.

c. List some actions you would have to take to create this imagined life.

d. Now examine each action you have listed, and, next to each one, describe the feelings holding you back from creating the life of your own imagination. It is helpful to focus on your breath, breathing heavily and slowly, to capture the feelings that you are describing.

e. What positive things would happen if you dared to take these actions despite the scary feelings? List them.

CHAPTER FOUR: Imagining a Life of Unity and Love: Getting Beyond Good and Evil, Success and Failure

19. **Secret Number Nineteen:** If anyone tells you that you are intrinsically deficient in any way, it is prudent to distrust their motivation and to keep their words from entering your heart. Disparagements in any form function to promote insecurity, fear, and a negative self-image. Internalizing negativity will produce an unhealthy dependency on others.

Some promote a disempowering self-image in others unwittingly. They unconsciously pass on what they have been told to believe and have internalized. Others seek to do so intentionally in order to gain dominance or to make you act in a certain way.

Feel free to lead a life of your own choosing, which comes from listening to an inner voice expressing wholeness, love, and appreciation. Appreciating your own self-worth will aid you in distinguishing between constructive advice and disempowering comments from others. It is important to recall your essence is one of love and everyone's journey is to tap into that spectacular essence that already exists within each one of us.

a. Can you recall being a child and receiving messages from an adult conveying to you a feeling of being less than, bad, or flawed in some way? Write down what was said to you and how that made you feel. (For me, being told I was born with original sin called me to question my self-worth.)

b. You can now play the role of a loving adult who wants to reassure the inner child in you who may have been devalued by others. Write down what you want to tell that child to build him/her up and make her/him feel whole. This type of loving language should set the standard of how you expect to be treated by others in your life. You will want to surround yourself with supportive people.

c. Be in silence, and feel that child within you. How does she/he feel when love is directed to her/him. Imagine her/him as a six-year-old sitting on your lap. Send your inner child warmth and tenderness.

d. When you are lying in bed and barely awake in the morning, make a habit of saying to yourself—all of you: adult and inner child—how much you love yourself. This is such a comforting experience.

You can make this easy by creating a reminder in your smartphone calendar to remind you each morning to say "I love you so much" to yourself. Believe me. This is incredibly empowering. I now have cultivated this as a habit, waking up with the thoughts of how much I love myself, and I often feel and think this at different points in my day. What a great habit to cultivate!

20. **Secret Number Twenty:** Refrain from judging as evil those who provoke feelings of pain or discomfort in you or whom you perceive as doing you wrong. It is far more productive to regard such "evildoers" as benefactors, because they create opportunities for personal empowerment by triggering your unresolved issues. Although they may hurt, these challenges can be appreciated. As with so many discomforts, sit with the experience, and be confident you can draw lessons from them. So often, what appears to be evil or malicious has a greater good if we give ourselves permission to recognize the good that will come out of it.

This is also an incredibly empowering posture to assume as we sidestep the temptation to enter victimhood. Assuming a posture of victimhood will inevitably reduce personal power. The power that comes from refraining from labeling as evil those who cause us discomfort can be experienced both at the personal level and at the community level, for instance, when we see ourselves as the victim of political actors.

Of course, if you are in a situation that is threatening, such as one of physical abuse or otherwise dangerous, remove yourself from such a situation and, if need be, defend yourself. After you are out of physical danger, allow a tranquil spirit to reemerge. After a state of inner quiet reemerges, you may learn how to avoid threats, how to develop healthier relationships, and how to find or create healthier situations.

a. Identify someone whom you believe caused you harm or offended you. Describe in some detail what this person did to make you believe they had committed something untoward to you.

b. Was this a surprise to you, or could you have seen it coming? What story were you telling yourself that prevented you from recognizing a potentially unhealthy situation and from acting to avoid it altogether? Describe this belief of yours in some detail.

c. From the present moment, look back at the situation, and ask yourself what important lessons have you learned from the experience. Write these lessons down. Then write about how you should think and act in a more loving way to yourself so as not to allow such a situation into your life in the future.

d. Describe the steps you intend to take to implement these lessons learned into your life. This is part of the promise to yourself to live a more empowered life.

e. Write down a thought of loving kindness toward yourself that will remind you of how precious and beautiful a person you are.

CHAPTER FIVE: The Inner Journey: Discovering the Power Within

21. **Secret Number Twenty-one:** You are beautiful beyond belief. Wouldn't it be a shame if you failed to appreciate your beauty and self-worth! There are different methods to help you experience your preciousness. You may have to pause in silence to witness your beautiful essence. This will allow you to rediscover the bounty of peace and joy that is available within you. Methods of discovering this inner wealth also include exploring art, yoga, meditation, silent walks, gardening, and more.

    As you glimpse your own worth and beauty, heed the call to return inwardly for that exquisite awareness of your own value. It may take some practice to break the habit of self-doubt. Stick with it, though. The joy you will feel will be immeasurable. And, in moments of self-doubt, accept the self-doubt with patience, allowing self-doubt to transform into confidence. Peace and joy will automatically manifest when this is done. Of this, you can always feel confident.

    a. Identify some ways you divert yourself from your inner feelings. List the feelings you may be avoiding.

b. Are there some activities or practices you already do that let you feel a sense of peace within you? Can you explain how this sense of peace comes about or where it springs from? One method of promoting a sense of peace that works for me is to breathe deeply into my belly and then my chest before slowly exhaling. What works for you?

c. Describe the feeling of peace you experience while you do these activities or practices. What might you do differently in your day to increase these activities or practices that have such a peaceful effect on you?

d. When you sense a troubling feeling such as fear, anger, sadness, or anxiety, accept it. In accepting your feelings, they will inevitably decrease in intensity. As this happens, gently remind yourself of the inner place of peace you have experienced, giving that place of peace permission to reenter your awareness. In time, engaging in these positive practices will turn into a new habit of accepting what is and of allowing your peaceful self to emerge into your awareness.

e. Oh! And, remember not to be critical of yourself for experiencing discomforting feelings. Always accept every feeling coming from within with understanding and self-compassion and without negative judgment. All feelings are valuable, as you can learn from them.

22. **Secret Number Twenty-two:** Yoga uses relaxation, breathing, and postures to smooth the ups and downs of emotional life. Those practicing yoga readily know how it calms and relaxes, eases and renews, and energizes and strengthens. One of the great benefits of yoga is discovering a comfortable peaceful state and the yoga poses that promote it. Feeling the quiet moments that come from yoga, you will lose the urge to escape from or push away whatever discomfort you experience. You become more confident of the treasure of positive emotional resources that lie within.

In the quiet that yoga promotes, you can observe how you respond to the world and find the opportunity to choose your response rather than to impulsively react. In enhancing your capacity to choose how to react to events in your world, yoga has a lot in common with formal meditative practice. Since this process involves increasing awareness of our inner talk and habitual patterns of belief and behavior, an important ingredient is to take an open and nonjudgmental attitude toward whatever you discover. Always treat yourself with self-compassion. (I can't say this enough.)

a.   Yoga practice allows you to enhance your personal power by bringing your body and mind together as a whole, developing a more harmonious, efficient, and creative relationship with yourself and your world. If you are not yet practicing yoga, you can begin now. You can do this by taking beginning yoga classes in a formal studio setting or following yoga instructions in online videos. If you already are a practitioner, continue to do so. Never feel you are competing with other yoga practitioners in undertaking poses. Wherever you are in your practice is just right.

b. Be sure you end your practice in a quiet relaxation pose often referred as *shavasana* which means corpse pose in the ancient Sanskrit language. During this pose, scan your body for tension and pain. Be aware of your breath, and send love to all those parts of your body that are tense or painful.

c. Keep this daily practice for a week, and in the next week, you will have the opportunity to grow in your awareness as your practice continues. If you are a person concerned about a lack of energy to perform life's productive tasks, there are yoga poses which will energize you at a physiological level.

d. Here are some links to free yoga videos by Esther Ekhart designed both to energize and to calm. I especially like Esther's approach.

Energizing practices:

    i. https://www.youtube.com/watch?v=VK4Aw DwGBL4

    ii. https://www.youtube.com/watch?v=iFNBZ6 BdmF8

    iii. https://www.youtube.com/watch?v=KWZiU LTVRzE

Calming practices:

    iv. https://www.youtube.com/watch?v=YBe1nz unHJ0

    v. https://www.youtube.com/watch?v=zC-izZtwjDY

23. **Secret Number Twenty-three:** The practice of art and of yoga produces physical and mental calming, increased relaxation, and reduced anxiety. Your worrying inner chatter will diminish, and you will likely even experience a heightened and healthy sexuality as your sense of creativity expands.

Engaging in yoga and art produces a shift in brain function, and there is considerable science to back up these observations. Perhaps, even more important than the validation of science, your own awareness of the enhanced states you can achieve will confirm the value of your practice. Such practices and the accompanying positive transformation in your mind-body relationship are essential mechanisms of personal empowerment. You will emerge from consistent practice much more the master of your own acts and with a more focused power that enables you to lead the responsible life intended for you.

For me, yoga practice often left me with a sense of peace and, for a long time, with a sense of sadness. I understood this sad feeling as yoga allowing a deep-seated sadness from my childhood to be released in a most constructive way. I suspect I am prone to store unacknowledged sadness in the form of acute muscle pain at trigger points. Consistent yoga practice helps me to release unrecognized sadness and to overcome my body's conditioned response to stress.

The secrets of personal empowerment presented in this book are designed to increase your self-awareness so as to reduce the perception of external stimuli as threatening and hence contribute to a less stress-filled life. It is not uncommon to interpret things not going as we would like as a form of punishment for our misguided sense of unworthiness. Getting to that point where we can remain neutral before events rather than labeling them as good or evil is a place of considerable personal power.

a. For this week, after your daily yoga practice, write down how you are feeling and what your body is experiencing. Try to reflect on how you felt before, during, and after the practice.

b. If your mind was active during your relaxation pose, describe in writing what you were telling yourself. This will help you increase your self-awareness throughout your day and over time. You will become more aware of any negative self-limiting talk you may be telling yourself as well as the positive self-talk you engage in. Make a list of the negative thoughts as well as the positive ones.

c. By acknowledging negative self-limiting talk, more empowering thoughts will emerge especially as you have committed to viewing yourself as worthy, being enough, and lovable. For every negative thought, use your imagination to create an alternative empowering thought as an alternative way of thinking. Write the empowering thought down. Over time, your positive, compassionate self-talk will increase and become your norm.

d. Remember how earlier in the Self-empowerment GPS, especially for Secrets Two and Four, you identified self-pity, "poor me" thoughts and thoughts of blaming others for your situation. Ask yourself if you still are continuing thoughts that are engaging in self-pity and blaming. If so, gently prompt yourself to leave these behind, reminding yourself you are now the master of your destiny.

24. **Secret Number Twenty-four:** The decision to acknowledge the peace, beauty, and truth within and to allow their expansion outward is a true act of freedom that releases untapped stores of creativity that remake the world and our experience of it. Making this decision to rediscover the place of peace, beauty, and truth within is the starting point for leading a responsible life, and once these are felt, you will be able to breathe forth a new world of peace and beauty of your own choosing. It is thus that we express our truth in and to the world.

Reshaping the world starts with the inward journey. The inevitable outward expression of that which you will find within constitutes the essential act of leading a responsible life. It will inevitably lead you to greater compassion for others, and you will become an advocate of justice for all. In delving inward and expressing outward, you will reach a state of maturity, of incredible authenticity, of wholesome integrity, and of enhanced personal power, and you will inspire others to do likewise.

a. Sit quietly for a few minutes. Allow any thoughts and feelings to emerge. It is best not to judge them but to merely accept them.

b. If you are feeling anxious, sad, or angry, remind yourself how beautiful and lovable you are. No one or anything can take away this essential awesome you. So often, it is easy to forget this truth about ourselves.

Describe in detail how lovable and beautiful you are. This type of reassuring self-love will more likely than not restore a sense of inner peace.

c. Now, imagine what your world would be like if you could gift the feeling of peace to others. Write it down. It's quite okay to focus on people and situations that are familiar to you. Describe how people you know might act differently if they operated from a place of peace. Or, you may want to imagine a society where a sense of peace and joy prevail. Describe what it would be like to live in such a community. How would people treat you? How would you treat others?

d. Identify people you know who may be operating from a place of self-doubt and shame. Write down what you would say to each of them to reassure them of their inner beauty and worthiness. You are making them a gift from your own sense of peace and worthiness. In so doing, you are transforming the world. Feel your personal power, and feel its potential for uplifting others.

25. Secret Number Twenty-five: Meditation is an important tool for enhancing your personal power. The utility of meditative practices derives in large measure from making yourself the observer of your own thoughts and feelings. Mastering the ability to observe the thoughts and feelings you create is an extremely useful tool for increasing your personal power.

Increasing your capacity for self-observation bestows great freedom upon you, because it sets the stage for choice, choosing how to respond emotionally to the world instead of just reacting, or choosing to let your mind rest in the powerful silence of no thought, or opting for thoughts that are positive and uplifting instead of negative and self-limiting. You can cease to be the servant of your own thought and be much more the master of your thoughts and hence your destiny. Thus, you become a creator rather than a slave or conformist.

It is also useful not to regard meditation practice as something difficult or only practiced in a set way. Meditative practice can be quite simple and down-to-earth. Quiet walks can be meditative; calming yoga poses can be meditative; writing a daily journal can be meditative; or you might find more formal sitting meditation productive. Feel free to experiment to see what works for you. Above all, be at ease, and certainly never feel you are inadequate in any way when you practice meditation. Your intent to grow in power will serve you well when you exercise patience and acceptance. Bringing patience and self-compassion to your meditative practice will fortify your capacity for self-observation and increase your reservoir of personal power—guaranteed!

Keep adopting uplifting, positive thoughts. Repetition will help you to replace the ingrained patterns of negative thought with more positive ways to look at any situation. (If you think some aspects of these exercises are somewhat repetitive, you are right. That's the point. You are creating a new habitual way of being in the world through repetition.)

a. As a morning empowerment exercise this week, not long after waking, take the time to write free flow for twenty minutes. By this, I mean write down whatever thoughts come to mind. Just let your thoughts and feelings flow uninterrupted. Incomplete sentences. Nonsensical grammar. Everything is permitted.

b. After three days of this, look back on your thoughts and identify any patterns. Are your thoughts self-critical, self-loving, fearful, or doubt-filled?

c. Continue writing for a few more days. And each day, go through the same exercise of examining your thoughts.

d. Next week, you will begin to look at how you might exercise your creativity to create more powerful thoughts, so don't lose your list of thoughts. You may need to refer to them. ☺

26. **Secret Number Twenty-six:** You command great power in understanding you created who you are. Perhaps, you did not do so consciously; as a child, you forged your self-identity, setting your limits as well as your spirit of adventurousness. The good news is that if as a child you could create your self-image and a life fulfilling that image it then stands to reason you as an adult have the creative potential to remake what you created in the first place.

As a child, you likely sought approval from those upon whom you were dependent. As an adult, you can develop a sense of self-confidence that lessens your emotional dependency on others. The creation of this emotional self-reliance is the creation of a new you. Stop the self-talk that derived from and reinforces an outdated image of yourself that was based on emotional dependency, and watch a new you be born from your insight, and experience the personal power that inevitably accumulates.

a. Take out the list of thoughts you wrote down during last week's exercise. Paying attention to your thoughts, your self-talk, will give you insight into your self-image. Self-image is what you think about yourself and what you tell yourself about what and who you are.

b. Now, ask yourself how your thoughts are determining the way you are perceiving the world. If you think your thoughts might be self-limiting, write down new ways of thinking that might increase your personal power. You can divide a sheet of paper with a line down the middle. On the left side, list your thoughts and behaviors that may be self-limiting. On the right side, for each limiting thought or behavior, write alternative ways of thinking or being in the world. Those on the right side are the new you. You may want to refer to the Hallmarks of an Empowered Person Table to stimulate your creativity. The table can be found at http://gregpirio.com/acquiring-personal-power-is-healthy-and-wise/.

c. Be patient with this process. Remember you are planting a seed that will take some time to become the giant oak you are.

d. If you are pursuing your hero's journey as part of a group of fellow travelers, share within the group what alternative ways of thinking are available for each other.

e. If, through this exercise, you feel you have been limiting yourself, accept the fact you are human and forgive yourself for being human. Be thankful for what new insights you have derived. Write your reflections, both forgiving and loving of yourself, down in an intimate note to yourself.

64

27. **Secret Number Twenty-seven:** When you have one of those days of uncertainty—when you feel walloped because the things you thought were predictable are in disarray and you just can't put them together or when fretting seems to be the only thing you can count on—in such moments, accept it all. Avoid self-criticism; avoid criticizing others. Just stay with the bundle, the messy bundle, you are experiencing.

Such moments are pregnant with possibilities. The new way and truth are merely incubating. If you can pause (feeling the moment, perhaps laughing), remind yourself you are in a moment of incubation. It's a pregnant moment. All will be revealed with patience and a position of nonjudgment. If you are wallowing in troubling thoughts and emotions of such moments, you will only prolong them, and the inspiration that can rise from within will be blocked or frustrated. Oh yes, and if you are wallowing, accept that as okay too. Commit the highest act of self-loving, which is total acceptance of wherever you are.

a. Identify someone whose qualities you admire. This person might be someone you know personally or someone you admire from a distance perhaps through the lens of history or a contemporary public figure.

   Write down reasons why you admire this person. Try to write down at least five reasons. If you can't come up with that number of reasons, that is okay too.

b. Now, imagine you are another person who is admiring you. What would this admiring person write about you? This is a good exercise for leaving self-criticism behind, and if these don't come all at once, that's okay. It may take some time for this self-appreciation to emerge, but you will become conscious of it.

c. Make a list of any additional positive qualities you do not yet see in yourself but you would like to embrace as your own. As a follow-up, just begin acting as this powerful person you really are but only now have come to acknowledge and to manifest.

28. **Secret Number Twenty-eight:** Try an experiment. When you feel a strong impulse to fulfill a craving, hold back from fulfilling it. You have nothing to lose by sitting in silence and then asking yourself if you are acting from a place of joy or if you are striving to achieve a feeling of happiness from acting out in a certain way or from performing certain actions. If the desire comes from an impulse to find happiness, remind yourself how beautiful and lovable you are. Acknowledge your self-worth. Over time, the acknowledgment will allow your natural sense of joy to emerge more strongly, and a sense of joy will become the standard of your life. Your desires will be healthier as you act from a place of peace and increasingly embrace yourself and the world in more loving ways. Over time, through repetition, this will become a positive empowering habit.

a. Take a few moments in silence to ask yourself the ways in which you may seek escape from uncomfortable feelings. Hints: comfort eating, using alcohol, sexual diversions, and many more.

b. If you are obese, your answer may have something to do with food.

c. If you often get high on substances including alcohol, ask yourself what feelings would likely come up if you refrained from using them. Does this occur in a social setting, or do you do this when you are alone? The next time you want to indulge, refrain and see what feelings emerge. Be sure to describe these feelings in writing to help you remember your process.

d. How else might you divert yourself from feeling?

e. For each discomforting feeling such as fear and anxiety you have identified, ask yourself what consequences there might be if you allowed feelings. Write these consequences down if you can truly identify any.

f. Then describe how the courageous you responds to discomforting feelings as you no longer seek escape from them.

CHAPTER SIX: The Life of Community: From Individualism to Richness

29. **Secret Number Twenty-nine:** Hope is a feeling that derives from a sense of inadequacy. Hope goes in tandem with fear. You can't have hope without having fear, and being fearful leaves you vulnerable to manipulation and exploitation as you reach for solutions outside of yourself.

It is important to realize there is nothing to hope for, because there is nothing lacking in you. There is no reason for doubting yourself. If you accept you are enough, there is nothing to hope for, nor are there reasons to be fearful. When you find yourself hoping for something or someone to make you feel better, the trick is to ask yourself what is the fear behind the hoping. In time, identifying the fear will help you to trust in yourself and to feel comfortable with yourself just as you are. Your sense of trust and confidence will grow and persist even at times when the outcome for which you have been hoping for may never happen.

In abandoning the habit of hoping for better, for more, or for success, you start more and more to concentrate activities not on achieving results that will earn you the admiration of others. Instead, you will increasingly obtain satisfaction from the social value, the rightness, and the truth of the activity itself.

In abandoning hope, the most important question to be asking becomes how can I best make a contribution to the world. What is the vision I have created for me and the world I inhabit? The highest reward for a person's productive activity is not what he/she obtains for it, but what he/she becomes by engaging in it. The purpose of life is to use one's own personal transformation to then help transform society. The journey of self-empowerment becomes the empowerment of others. But, be sure you don't sacrifice yourself by seeking to transform others. Others will be transformed by experiencing your empowered presence.

Likewise, in abandoning the hope of finding romantic love as a rescue from loneliness, we will look for friends who will support us and validate our positive sense of self. The people who can validate us best are those we can see as equals and with whom there can be mutual affection, trust, loyalty, and acceptance. Such people give us the kind of validation that reinforces our sense of self-confidence, especially when we might be doubting ourselves.

Self-love and emotional self-reliance replace the disempowering paradigm of hoping. Abandon hope and embrace confidence!

a. List five luxury possessions you don't have that would make you happier if you were to acquire them. Next to each item, describe how they would make you happy.

b. Now, if you had them, ask yourself how possessing them would increase your sense of self-worth. Write down what comes up, also asking yourself how your sense of personal power will be enhanced. How does possessing these objects contribute to a better world.

c. If you are looking for a romantic relationship, describe the type of relationship you may be longing for, if indeed you are. Are you looking for a cure from loneliness or for someone who will encourage your personal growth?

d. Describe what would happen to you if you never found that right person who, you believe, would make you happy.

e. Ask yourself what kind of person you would be if you stopped wanting, hoping, for the love of your life. And, if you were to find that right person, ask yourself what kind of person you would be.

f. What steps could you take to release the joy that already abides within you? To help you think about this, in a quiet meditative-like moment, think about all the qualities you have that you can be thankful for.

g. Write "I am thankful that I am ___________." Repeat this phase for each quality or personal characteristic you come up with. Be exhaustive in your reflection on personal qualities to be thankful for.

h. Being thankful for who you are helps to neutralize a sense of inadequacy and to build your sense of confidence. Being thankful for who you are will release your joy.

30. **Secret Number Thirty:** A paradox of self-empowerment can be seen between the call to love oneself and the idea one can only be fully realized in community. This duality resolves itself, however, when we have the courage to look directly into our own soul and allow feelings even uncomfortable feelings. It is then that our sense of individuality ebbs away. We become connected to others in ways that are difficult to articulate. Distinctions between you and me, between them and me, melt away. An authentic sense of healthy belonging, if not of oneness, avails itself if we so allow.

And the opposite holds true. When we allow the pain of others to enter us, when we no longer put up defenses to protect ourselves from the frightening prospect we are vulnerable to pain, insecurity, and loss like that which the refugee, the dispossessed, and fretting people feel, we see our common humanity; we see ourselves in them. We too become vulnerable; we become one in the inevitable vulnerability of human existence.

Paradoxically, when we establish this community, we no longer feel impoverished; we no longer feel lacking. In this community of vulnerable individuals, we experience abundance, self-worth, dignity, and joy. In the isolation of rabid individualism, we feel impoverished, always lacking, and grasping for things to make us feel adequate. And, we create a world of winners and losers.

The truth is that we flourish only in community.

Community is all around us. To help strengthen one's sense of community, follow the exercises below. They are designed to help improve appreciation of how we are so embedded in community and interconnected literally to everyone on the planet. It is important to remain aware of how self-empowerment is realized as part of a community. While your individual effort is at the core of your journey, your self-realization occurs in dialog with community. Healthy self-empowerment also breaths wholesome life into community.

a. Take a gratitude walk at the beginning of this week. This walk consists of examining many objects that surround us. These can be the vegetation, the sky and all aspects of mother nature. Imagine how the air that you breath also sustained ancient civilizations.

b. While strolling, move your attention beyond the natural world and focus on the human-made objects. This might be the sidewalk under your feet, the drains that collect the run off from rain, the buildings that are home to your neighbors, the electric grid, the schools and so much more. Ponder the people who made all this possible – the workers, the designers, the taxpayers, the people paying rents and mortgages. Sense how you are connected to others in a web of community.

c. Take a couple of these gratitude tours this week, and, in your daily journal, write down how you imagine these people to be who have created the world you inhabit. Describe how you imagine them to be – the farmworkers who harvested the food you eat, the truck drivers who brought them to the grocery stores, the people who produced the books on your shelf, and on and on.

d. Imagine how their lives and feelings. What about their loved ones? What fears they may have? How might they be the same or different from you?

e. As you are writing these thoughts and feelings down, sense your own journey of self-empowerment. Can you imagine gifting to them the peace and joy you have come to feel through your own self-empowerment?

f. From a sense of oneness with others in this community you have described above, imagine ways that the self-empowered you can contribute to the healthy well-being of others. Write these down.

31. **Secret Number Thirty-one:** Worrying is an unparalleled opportunity to take notice of disempowering self-talk and for challenging the harmful things you are telling yourself about yourself. When you catch yourself worrying, pay attention to the details of your self-talk. Write down the thoughts that underlie the feeling of worry. Examine them. Become familiar with them. Refrain from criticizing yourself for having them. Accept them. You will notice a veil being lifted, and you will experience a peaceful space even though this feeling may be fleeting and tentative at first.

From a space of peace, however small it may be, grant yourself the blessing of kindness and love. If you sense an inner child within you, that child—the younger you—may have felt unloved, neglected, or even abused. Send kindness and love to that child, reassuring him/her you are in charge and will be caring for him/her. Resolve to act in loving ways to yourself. With time and patience and practice, the inner child will heal and know the adult you is reliable. Your worrying will lessen.

Over time, as you bestow loving kindness on yourself, you will increasingly use thoughts of self-love as a motivation to accomplish activities you are interested in. Worrying will no longer be seen as a motivator to do something. You will be telling yourself "I plan to undertake activities because this is a way of loving myself." This is an inevitable transformation over time. Nonetheless, whenever you may feel worrying coming on, you can transfer the energy that upsets you into a reminder to bestow loving kindness unto yourself. Your sense of faith and confidence will grow.

a. Throughout this week, take a mental note whenever you catch yourself worrying, and as soon as you can, make a written note of it in your journal so you don't forget it.

b. Find time to describe the thoughts you had for each of these instances of worry you have noted. Then, next to each worrying thought, write down a counter, self-affirming positive thought that comes from a place of inner loving kindness.

c. Imagine the child within you, and counsel you, the child, about her/his worth and lovability. Tell that child not to worry, as you are the adult who will solve problems and take care of her/him. Write a letter to your inner child telling her/him how much you love her/him.

d. Communicate to yourself in this loving and kindly way all week long and for as long as possible. Indeed, do this for the rest of your life.

CHAPTER SEVEN: The Road to Kakamega and the Ultimate Secret of Self-empowerment—Self-love

32. **Secret Number Thirty-two:** To let your inner joy emerge, it is important not to allow anyone to prey on your sense of inadequacy or even to try to increase it. Such actions are a form of abuse and exploitation. The secret is to understand you are already beautiful and whole beyond imagination. I wish that confidence for you as should everyone.

In my American culture, this type of abuse and exploitation is pervasive. In the public arena, for example, we are heavily programmed to believe consumption of products will deliver happiness to us. Industries exist to sell us some form of happiness. Typically, they offer to improve us so we are more acceptable or desirable. Possessing an object is bound to give us joy, they promise.

Just look at how the advertisements on TV offer us commodities with the promise of overcoming our flaws. Toothpaste will make our smiles more appealing and attractive to potential lovers. Automobiles are pitched as a way to become more powerful and sexy. And, there are the clothes, cosmetics, weight reduction plans, and physical fitness gyms to make us acceptable to others. For years, a global soft drink company explicitly adopted an advertising campaign that assured happiness through the consumption of its products. Seeking happiness through consumption is a form of addictive behavior that keeps us away from the authentic place of peace and joy that resides within us.

The secret is to embrace your inner beauty and let it radiate out to the world like an infectious substance. Realize your inner beauty will help others understand their own self-worth. Act from a place of confidence that says you are enough just as you are.

a. On a piece of paper, write down a list of your physical defects, if you feel you have any, and how you would like to look. Most people can find something such as bigger biceps, six-pack abs, bigger/smaller boobs, thinner thighs, etcetera. Now, take the paper and tear it up into small pieces and throw it into a wastebasket.

b. Then, go to a mirror and tell yourself how beautiful/handsome you are, just as you are. If you have a full-length mirror, admire yourself fully naked in front of the mirror.

c. As you look in the mirror admiring who you are, remind yourself how important it is for you to care for this amazing person you see before you. Recommit to taking care of this lovely being standing in the mirror through healthy eating and proper exercise.

d. Write down in your journal what thoughts went through your mind as you gazed upon the magnificence that is you. If you have any negative perceptions of your beauty, next to the negative thoughts, write alternative, empowering thoughts such as:

> i. I was beautiful, I am beautiful, and I will be beautiful forever.
> ii. I look beautiful, and I speak beautiful. Beauty is my nature and my calling.
> iii. Every cell in my body is beautiful, and I radiate that outward into the world.
> iv. I am beautiful as well as healthy.

e. Do this every day for this week and for as long as it takes for you to truly realize your beauty.

f. Truly loving yourself means you are committed to healthy living. As you commit or recommit to living a healthy life, envision a life of healthy eating and exercise for yourself. There are websites to help you design and follow a plan for developing a healthy lifestyle. Over time, you will be able to develop your own plan as your knowledge of healthy habits increase.

g. For help with a healthy living plan, you can consult a Mayo Clinic offering at https://diet.mayoclinic.org/diet/home/

Or consult a Harvard University site at https://www.health.harvard.edu/nutrition/the-harvard-medical-school-6-week-plan-for-healthy-eating-copy

33. Secret Number Thirty-three: Fear is the fall from your state of confidence. It takes courage to stay on the course of exploration and growth you have set out on. Nevertheless, there will be moments when you may once again experience fear as you dare to enter unchartered territory. Such moments of fear will likely feel a bit unsettling because you have actually developed a habit of viewing yourself and your world from a place of confidence.

That you have come to experience fear again on your journey is actually a positive sign. Congratulate yourself on this new experience of fear. It means you have dared to be on unchartered territory and have assumed responsibility for your fate. Whether you find yourself in a fearful or confident state, you are always worthy and enough. No state of mind or uncomfortable feeling can ever deprive you of the exalted birthright of being enough and worthy.

Experiencing fear anew will also likely put you into that old place of self-pity, of blaming others, and of spiritual paralysis you have left behind. Say to yourself "I am too beautiful, unique, deserving, and downright too awesome to undercut myself by going back to these old disempowering habits." Personal greatness already and always exists within you. Be patient with your fear; patience—that act of loving kindness to yourself—in itself will return you to the experience of your personal greatness and confidence. Count on it!

a. For several days this week, every time you feel fear or anger (Anger is a reflexive action to the experience of fear.), write down what you are fearful of and the negative thoughts going through your mind in those fearful moments.

    i. For example, you may write: "I am fearful that __________ will happen because I am _____________."

    ii. The fears you may list could reflect routine fears like negative consequences for being late for something or big fears like something catastrophic could happen. All fears are valid for this exercise.

b. At the end of the week, divide a piece of paper with a line down the middle from top to bottom. On the left side, begin listing the fears you became aware of. On the right side, next to each fear, write down a positive quality about yourself that can never be taken away from you.

c. At the end, write two paragraphs designed to comfort the inner child within you who may have felt fearful. Use the qualities you have written down to remind your inner child of his/her intrinsic lovability. Love that child. Indeed, love all children.

34. **Secret Number Thirty-four:** The notions of success and failure are cultural constructs that can be embraced or discarded because they are a reality that exists only in our minds. And, it may be advantageous to imagine a life not framed by these concepts because our personal happiness—even the future of the planet—may depend upon us finding alternative paradigms for being productive and responsible in our world. The importance placed on success and failure is the source of needless confusions, pain, and suffering at a personal level, and might not the impulse to be seen as successful be behind the economic forces driving climate change that is threatening human existence on the planet?

These twin concepts of success and failure play on a common and deep-rooted fear I am inadequate as I am. This sense of inferiority produces a craving for recognition and prestige as a way of proving to ourselves we are worthy. The trap of success and failure lies in using external cues as measurements of self-worth, as a way of compensating for that which we sense to be lacking within. In such a scenario, our sense of self-worth comes to depend on what we imagine to be the judgment of others.

Tapping into the innate creativity in all of us is frankly a lot more fun way to approach work and industry than is the pursuit of success. Trusting in one's creativity and manifesting it into the world is a lot like being a child left to imagine and play out the role of hero, facing danger and adversity, or from a hero's position of doubt, displaying courage, bravery, or self-sacrifice in a positive way. (See Beyond Success and Failure at http://gregpirio.com/beyond-success-and-failure/)

a. Make a list of people, situations, accomplishments, or anything else that gives meaning to your life and for which you are thankful. Then, next to each item, describe how it gives meaning to your life. You might write something like "I appreciate this because it makes me feel ___________." Ask yourself what allows you to attract such wonderful things in your life.

b. Then, focus on some things you would like to accomplish but have hesitated to pursue because either you have set out and made some "mistakes" or you fear failing. For each of them, describe what is holding you back from moving forward. Describe what fears are at work. For each item you would like to accomplish, outline a brief plan for moving forward to realizing this vision. And, begin to implement the steps with the knowledge there is no such thing as failure. Also, keep a look out for unexpected opportunities that will surely emerge as you act from a place of confidence.

c. In a previous exercise, you have set your smartphone calendar to send you an "I love you" reminder each morning. Now, set up a daily reminder to reach you around bedtime, reminding you to be thankful for who you are. A good message is "Thanking you, (your name), for just being you."

35. **Secret Number Thirty-five:** The achievement and practice of self-love inexorably leads to a greater sense of our shared humanity and how the inner peace and joy that is experienced radiates effortlessly into the world. By understanding others on the level of our common humanity, we are able to spread the message of self-love and create space for others to love themselves. This radiated power manifests in its simplest way in how we interact with others, showing caring and concern as well as encouragement to all, especially to others who may be troubled or fearful.

This radiated love becomes the basis for promoting social justice within your world. Self-love leads to positive community engagement and caring. Self-love inevitably leads to confidence and positive social engagement. It will happen.

And, when caring comes from a position of self-love, you will be able to set healthy boundaries and learn not to overextend yourself. Always remember to check in with your inner feelings to make sure you are not needlessly sacrificing yourself. As your personal power and greatness grow, as your commitment to self-love grows, your manifestation of love will be assuredly healthy.

This week, pay attention to the disempowered qualities you perceive in others.

a. Pick a political figure who appears uncaring (perhaps dismissive and condescending) toward people in vulnerable circumstances. In your journal, describe their behavior and imagine how his/her childhood upbringing might have contributed to the development of his/her disdainful and condescending attitude toward those in more vulnerable circumstances. Imagine how they should have been treated differently as a child so as to develop a greater sense of loving kindness to self and toward others.

b. Pick someone you know personally who has addictive tendencies, be it drug or alcohol abuse, an eating disorder, or compulsive buying. Describe what feelings they are likely to be covering up or seeking to escape through their damaging behavior. Write a paragraph or two reminding them of their beauty, brilliance, and essential worthiness.

c. Search the internet for a story about a refugee fleeing his/her homeland where there may be poverty or violence. Describe what they must feel when the country of safe haven accepts them and what he or she likely feels if the country rejects them, deporting them to an unsafe land.

36. **Secret Number Thirty-six:** It is possible, indeed fitting, to give direction to the seemingly boundless loving energy that emanates from within as your self-loving grows. You can direct the manifestation of this positive energy in ways inspired by your vision of a world of greater peace and joy. This is designing your energy's intervention into the world in ways that go beyond its spontaneous manifestation. This occurs because you are already experiencing such an empowered state of being and are realizing its potential for others.

In accepting responsibility for directing this flow of energy, all those who have experienced a spiritual awakening and have committed to undertaking the journey of personal empowerment are positioned to create a world of their own choosing—much like an artist paints on a canvas. Indeed, you really have no choice but to act creatively in the world as you accumulate personal power through self-empowerment, in part, because you have set out on a trajectory of assuming responsibility and of abandoning the old, worn-out habit of blaming others.

Your capacity for assuming responsibility will only grow in strength by acting responsibly. The more you exercise responsibility, the more your capacity for nurturing a community of caring people will be fortified. As the contagion of self-love spreads, so does the societal sense of security, and all will benefit from this.

a. Create a vision of how your loving energy may impact the lives of others. You decide where you would like it to flow—in your family, in a religious institution, toward those suffering from discrimination or persecution, toward refugees, through civic engagement and political action, toward the homeless, through spiritual coaching, and on and on.

b. After you have decided how you want to create a more loving and caring community, describe in your journal how you imagine your intervention may make a difference in the lives of others. What would that look like?

Afterword: Glimpsing the Mystical Experience

I want to express my gratitude to you for having selected both *Outside Eden's Gate: The Secrets of Self-empowerment* and its companion guide, *Your Self-empowerment GPS* as well as for having taken important steps toward your personal empowerment.

In *Outside Eden's Gate,* I indicated self-love is the prize to be found at the end of the hero's journey. Through your considerable effort and dedication in following the steps laid out in *Your Self-empowerment GPS*, you are likely already experiencing a wholehearted appreciation of yourself and are practicing the art of self-loving. Continue your commitment to *"Dare to be you; Dare to Love Yourself."*

Make a promise to yourself to stay on this path you have chosen. The *GPS* guide remains a wholesome touchstone for you. So, please return to secrets in the book and the guide (as well as the exercises) to remind yourself of the attitudes, beliefs and behaviors enabling you to be truly you—the confident, courageous, creative and competent you. I suggest you return to the secrets and exercises at least within two-months of having completed the self-empowerment course and as often as you like. Revisiting the *Your Self-empowerment GPS* will reinforce your positive habits and be a reminder of the progress you have made, providing further encouragement to continue your personal empowerment journey.

As part of your self-loving experience, encourage others to follow the *Self-empowerment GPS*. After all, we want to see a world filled with empowered people. Imagine all the people, like you, living in a world of peace and joy!

Also, be prepared for a surprise beyond the "prize of self-love" at the end of the hero's journey. This surprise consists of a sense of interconnectedness—a sense of oneness—with all. This feels mystical in how it inspires mystery, awe, and fascination. You likely already have had your own experience with this spiritual dimension while on your self-empowerment journey. I often have glimpses of this awesome dimension and have yet to find the language to adequately describe it. Perhaps, it can be best expressed through poetry and other art forms as well as through lovemaking.

I will gladly share with you my new discoveries as I learned best how to express the feelings that come from this awesome, seemingly mystical experience. So, keep coming back to www.gregpirio.com. I want to keep sharing with you what I discover. And, please share your understandings with others so that together we can create a more loving world.

www.ingramcontent.com/pod-product-compliance
Lightning Source LLC
Chambersburg PA
CBHW070813170726
48000CB00017B/876